*"My Cooking"*

❖

# WEST-AFRICAN COOKBOOK

# "My Cooking"
# WEST-AFRICAN
# COOKBOOK

by
Dokpe Lillian Ogunsanya

"My Cooking"
West-African Cookbook
Dupsy Enterprises
(512) 990-9508
P.O.Box 80841
Austin, Texas 78708-0841
U.S.A.

E-mail: dupsy@msn.com

First Edition 1998

ISBN 0-9662730-0-1

BOOK DESIGN & TYPOGRAPHY BY
JOHN FRANZETTI
AUSTIN, TEXAS

PHOTOGRAPHS BY
STEPHANIE HUEBINGER
AWARD WINNING PHOTOGRAPHER
AUSTIN, TEXAS

# Dedication

*T*his book is dedicated to
Almighty God,
for his grace and mercy;
My Husband,
who supported me enormously;
My Parents,
who left me a legacy;
My Family and Friends,
who in one way or the other encouraged
and contributed to the success of this book;
And most especially to
the readers of this book,
thank you!

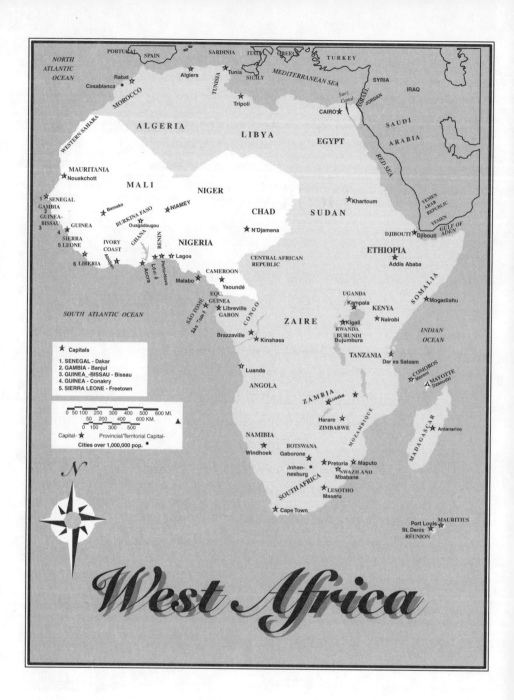

# West Africa

WEST AFRICAN COOKBOOK

# Contents

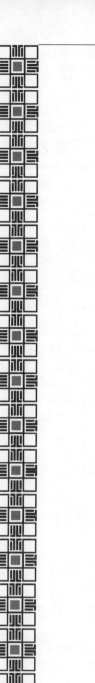

## 51
## Snacks and Deserts

# 79
# Ethnic Specialties

# 87
# Beverages

# 92
# Glossary

# 95
# Index

# 100
# Your Favorite Recipes

# INTRODUCTION

$\mathcal{A}$frica is a continent rich in natural resources and food is no exception. The continent is blessed with a wide variety of food items. Food preparation and cooking plays an important role in the African tradition. It is an expression of the culture. Many Africans believe that "the way to people's heart is through their stomach." A good cook wins a lot of "hearts". Africans take a lot of pride in food preparation and cooking - to them it is as imperative as knowing how to perform some of the ceremonial rites.

"My Cooking" is comprised of cuisines originating from Nigeria in West-Africa. These cuisines are common all over West-Africa though prepared differently and are sometimes called different names due to language and other factors. I feel that there is a need for a cookbook with simple but authentic recipes which introduces both Africans and non-Africans to the variety of African cuisines. To Africans, particularly Nigerians, this book may serve as a reminder of forgotten dishes and to others it will be a pleasant adventure.

As with American dishes, there are many ways to food preparation and cooking - most of the recipes included in this book are favorites of "My Cooking" - a taste of authenticity. Traditional dishes vary from tribe to tribe. Many African traditional dishes are characterized by the use of various seasonings and hot pepper. There is an idiomatic expression among West-Africans that "pepper is the staff of life and the man that eats no pepper is weak". This is one of the reasons why most Africans favor hotly spiced food. There is also the belief by some Africans that pepper serves as a cleansing system to the body, improves the taste and flavor of food and serves as natural food preservative. "My

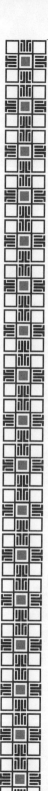

Cooking" calls for a moderate use of pepper; this can however be increase or decrease according to one's taste. The recipes in this book aid in making some of the common foods that can be eaten by almost anyone. I have selected easy to follow recipes and avoided recipes that calls for ingredients that are not readily available. A lot of the ingredients are well known here in the United States and generally around the world, though used differently. Most African meals are usually made up of one course - the book features main meals, snacks, deserts, ethnic specialties, and beverages. Various dishes can however be combined into a meal of several courses or buffet. Vegetables and fruits should always be included as side dishes when necessary. Stewing is the chief method of cooking; however, baking, roasting and frying are also very common.

The secret of a successful use of this book is to read through the recipe you want to prepare, check the glossary for reference and have all the necessary ingredients ready before you start cooking. Most of the ingredients are readily available at the local grocery stores or ethnic stores that sell African food products. Please feel free to write me if you have any question or problem locating the ingredients.

I am much indebted to my mother, her friends and neighbors in Lagos, Nigeria for introducing me to the art of cooking in my early years. "It indeed takes the whole village to raise a good cook."

My formal education and professional career are in the areas of Public Administration (M.P.A.), Computer Science and Mass Communications. Cooking and Business are however my passion. I sincerely hope that "My Cooking" becomes a favorite in your homes as you serve and enjoy the food prepared from the recipes in the book!

*Bon Appetit!*

# MAIN DISHES
# &
# ACCOMPANIMENT

# Tropical Fried Rice with Baked Chicken

1½ pounds of Rice
1  fryer Chicken, cut into 4 parts
1  cup of small Shrimp parboiled
1  cup of Vegetable Oil
1  cup of chopped Carrot
1  cup of Sweet Corn
1  cup of Green Peas
1  large size Onion (chopped)
1  small Onion (sliced)
2  large size Green Bell Pepper (chopped)
1  large size Red Bell Pepper (chopped)
1  large size Tomato (chopped)
3  Maggi or Bouillon cubes
1  tablespoon of chopped Garlic
1  teaspoon of Curry Powder
½  teaspoon of Thyme
½  teaspoon of Ginger Powder
   Salt to taste and pinch of Garlic Powder

*B*oil rice until medium soft and drain excess water. Wash and clean chicken. Season with a pinch of curry powder, thyme, garlic powder and salt to taste. Parboil chicken covered in a cooking pot for about 15 minutes. Skim off the chicken fat and leave only the stock. Put The chicken in a baking pan and add the sliced onion. Bake on medium heat for about 15 minutes or until golden brown. Heat oil in a large pot until sizzling hot. Add chopped onion, garlic, shrimp, tomato, green pepper, red pepper and carrot. Cook and stir on medium heat for about 5 minutes, then add curry, thyme, ginger, maggi(bouillon) cubes and salt to taste. Cover pot and cook for about 10 minutes or until carrot becomes tender. Add rice and stir for even distribution of flavor. Allow to simmer for about 15 minutes and add corn and peas. Stir and add more salt if necessary. Serve with the baked chicken on the side.

Makes 4 servings .

# Jollof Rice

1½  pounds of Rice
1    cup of cubed Beef
½    cup of Cooking Oil
1    14½ oz. can of Stewed Tomatoes
1    large Onion (¼ chopped)
1    medium size Red Bell Pepper
2    Maggi or Bouillon cubes
1    teaspoon of chopped Garlic
1    teaspoon of Thyme
½    teaspoon of Curry Powder
     Salt to taste
1    pkg. frozen Carrots & Green Peas for garnishing

Parboil rice and drain excess water. Clean and boil beef covered
for about 12 to 15 minutes. Blend or grind the pepper, stewed
tomatoes and ¼ of the onion. Heat the oil in a large cooking pot
until sizzling hot. Add the chopped ¼ onion and garlic. Pour in
the blended ingredients. Add maggi(bouillon) cubes, thyme,
curry and salt to taste. Add cubed beef. Pour and stir the rice
into the pot and cook on low heat for about 15 minutes or until
cooked. Cover tightly and stir at intervals to blend in the flavors.
Follow the direction on package to prepare the frozen carrots and
peas or parboil sliced raw carrots and peas. Garnish rice with carrots and peas just before serving.

Serve with meat, fish or salad.

Makes 4 to 6 servings.

# Coconut Rice

1   lb of Rice
3   cups of Coconut Milk
½   cup of parboil Shrimp
1   cup of cubed Beef
2   Maggi or Bouillon cubes
1   small size Tomato (chopped)
1   small size Green Pepper (chopped)
1   small size Onion (chopped)
1   pinch of Dry Pepper
    Salt to taste

*P*arboil rice. Clean and boil beef for about 10 to 15 minutes or until tender. Add salt and 3 slices of onion to taste. Boil coconut milk for about 8 minutes and add the cooked meat, shrimp and maggi(bouillon) cubes. Add rice and cook on low heat for about 30 minutes. Stir in tomatoes, green pepper, onion, dry pepper and salt to taste. Reduce heat and simmer for about 10 minutes till rice is soft and fluffy.

Makes 4 servings.

# Ebe

## (Shrimp Potatoes Pottage)

8   large Potatoes
1   lb. medium size Shrimp parboiled
1   14½ oz. can of Stewed Tomatoes
½   cup of Vegetable Oil
1   small size Onion (chopped)
½   lb of Sugar
½   teaspoon of dry ground Red Pepper
2   pinches of Garlic
2   pinches Curry
2   pinches Thyme
    Salt to taste

Peel and cut potatoes into large cubes and put in a large sauce pan. Cover with water, add sugar, 3 pinches of salt and bring to boil until potatoes become tender (avoid overcooking). Drain out excess water. Crush or mash stewed tomatoes in a mixing bowl. In a medium size sauce pan or skillet heat oil until sizzling hot. Add onion, tomatoes, pepper and 2 pinches of each spice. Allow to cook for about 5 minutes. Add parboiled shrimp and allow to cook for another 6 minutes stirring occasionally. Pour into the pot with potatoes and stir with a wooden spoon "mashing" some of the potatoes. Cook for few minutes and cool before serving.

Serve with baked or fried fish.

Makes 4 servings.

# Quick Lunch
# Corned Beef Sandwich

8   slices of Wheat or Regular Bread
4   oz Corned Beef(canned-ready to eat)
2   tablespoon of soft Butter or Margarine
1   hard boiled Egg (sliced)
1   pinch of Black Pepper
    crispy Lettuce for garnishing

*M*ix butter or margarine with corned beef and black pepper. Spread a thin layer of mixture on a slice of bread, add some lettuce, add another layer of mixute and top with 2 slices of boiled egg. Cover with another slice of bread and slice across to form a triangle.

Serve with your favorite fruits

Makes 2 servings.

# African Omelette

4   large Eggs
⅓   cup of Cooking Oil
⅓   cup of chopped Green Pepper
⅓   cup of chopped Onion
⅓   cup of diced Tomatoes
⅓   of caned Corned Beef or Sardines
2   pinches of Black Pepper
    Salt to taste

Mix eggs. Heat oil until hot. Saute all ingredients in oil except egg mixture. Reduce heat and add egg mixture. Cook for few minutes.

Serve with bread, pancake, boiled yam or plantain.

Makes 4 servings.

# Homemade Pancakes

2   cups of All Purpose Flour
2   large Eggs
1   cup of Milk
3   tablespoon of Sugar
2   pinches of Salt
1   pinch of Baking Powder
½   cup of Water
½   cup Cooking Oil
    dash of Nutmeg or Ginger (optional)

*B*eat eggs, mix with milk and water. Add sugar and salt. Mix well, add flour, baking powder and nutmeg or ginger. Stir until flour is moistened. Batter will be slightly lumpy. Pour oil into a frying pan and heat until hot. Reduce heat. Pour (about ¼ of cup per pancake) batter into frying pan or hot greased griddle. Cook for few minutes until bottom surface becomes light golden brown. Turn, cook and brown other side.

Serve with toppings of your choice

Makes 6 servings.

# Tropical Vegetable Salad

(This is a very colorful and splendor dish!)

1 can of Salmon or 10 oz. of cooked Fish (optional)
1 can of Baked Beans (16oz)
5 hard boiled Eggs (sliced)
1 large size green Leaf Lettuce
1½ cup of package of frozen Carrots and Peas
1 large Cucumber (sliced)
2 large fresh Tomatoes (sliced)
1 large of White Onion (sliced)
1 large Green Pepper (sliced)
1 small sliced Beetroot (Red Beet) (optional )
1 cup of diced Pineapple
¼ cup of Peanuts (chopped or broken into smaller bits) (optional)
1 teaspoon of Apple Cider Vinegar
2 pinches of Black Pepper
  Salad Dressing
  Salt to taste

Clean and wash lettuce in a solution of water and 1 teaspoon of apple cider vinegar to give the lettuce a clean crispy texture. Flake and remove bones from fish (remove fat and drain out sauce if using canned fish). Place onion in boiling water, add 3 pinches of salt and cover for 2 minutes. Pour in a colander to drain out water. Place frozen carrots and peas in boiling water, add 2 pinches of salt and cover for 3 minutes. Pour in a colander to drain out water. Set each bowl of ingredients side by side in form of an assembly line. On a large flat plate or tray, arrange ingredients starting with a bed of lettuce. Make sure that each layer has a combination of all ingredients. Sparingly add salad dressing in between layers. This should make about 2 or 3 layers depending on the size of plate or tray. Cover and put in the refrigerator for about 1 hour before serving.
Serve with extra salad cream on the side.

Makes 6 to 8 servings.

# Moin Moin

## (Moyin Moyin) (Bean Cake or Steamed Blackeyed Pea)

3   cups of dehulled (skinless) Blackeyed Pea Paste or
    powder (see glossary)
¼   lb parboiled Shrimp
2   hard boiled Eggs
3   oz of Corned Beef or Chopped Ham
1   cup of Vegetable Oil
1   medium size Onion (chopped)
1   tablespoon of dry ground Red Pepper or
1   large Red Bell Pepper (ground)
1   teaspoon of Tomato Paste
3   Maggi or Bouillon cubes
1   pinch of Curry Powder
2   cups of warm Water
    Salt to taste

𝒫ut blackeyed pea paste in a large mixing bowl. Add onion,
pepper and corned beef. Mix and stir in vegetable oil. Add curry
and maggi(bouillon) (disolved in little hot water). Mix properly.
Cut aluminum foil into rectangels(5"x 8"). Fold in half(4"x 4"),
double fold the edges on the two sides that are on either side of
the fold, leaving one side open to form a pocket. Use a scoop or
large cooking spoon to put the mixture into foil pockets. Baking
or steaming cups may also be used. Garnish with shrimp and
slices of the boiled eggs. Double fold the remaining edge closed.
Steam  tightly covered until firm for about 50 minutes.

Serve with rice dishes for parties or as a side dish with fried
plaintain.

Makes 8 servings.

# Akara

### (Fried Blackeyed Peas Fritters (African Hush Puppies))

2   cups of Blackeye Pea Paste (see glossary)
1   small chopped Onion
½   teaspoon of dry ground Red Pepper
    Salt to taste
    Vegetable Oil for deep frying

Whip the paste.  Mix the paste with onion, pepper and salt.
Add a little bit of warm water (the mixture should remain thick).
Continue mixing until mixture becomes about the consistency of
a thick cake batter.  Heat oil (about 400°).  Use tablespoon or
scoop to drop the batter into the hot oil.  Fry until golden brown
(there may be a need to flip the batter on each side to obtain even
color).  Drain excess oil.

May be served as snack or as a side dish.

Makes 10 servings.

# Seasoned Blackeyed Peas

1  lb of Blackeyed Peas
½  cup of Cooking Oil
1  medium size Onion
2  medium size fresh Tomatoes
1  small Green Bell Pepper
1  pinch of Curry Powder
   Salt to taste
   Water

Boil blackeyed peas in plenty of water on high heat for about 15 minutes.  Salt to taste.  Reduce heat to simmer and cook for about 45 minutes or until peas becomes tender.  Slice or cube onion, tomatoes and green pepper.  Saute onion for about 3 minutes, add tomatoes, pepper, curry and salt.  Cook for about 8 minutes.  Add blackeyed peas and cook for about 5 minutes.

Serve with Dodo (fried plantain).

Makes 5 servings.

# Rice and Beans

2   cups of Rice
1½ cups of Blackeyed Peas
    Water
    Salt to taste

*I*mmerse blackeyed peas in water and salt and parboil for about 20 minutes. Add rice and more water. Cook on low heat for about 20 minutes or until rice becomes tender.

Serve with fish or beef stew and Dodo (fried ripe plantain) on the side.

Makes 6 servings.

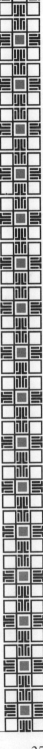

# Dodo

### (Fried Ripe Plantain)

4   fingers of ripe Plaintain (bright yellow and soft)
    Vegetable Oil for deep frying
    Salt (optional) to taste

*P*eel plaintain and slice into desired shapes (diagonal, round, slant oval or small chunks in form of cubes). Season lightly with salt if desired. Heat oil till hot (about 400°F). Fry plaintain till light brown. Avoid over cooking, for it can easily get burnt. Remove plaintain from frying pan or pot and drain out excess oil. Excess oil may be drained on paper towel.

Plantain can be served as a light meal with stew, as a side dish, or use to garnish.

Makes 4 servings.

# Boiled Plaintain

4  fingers of ripe Plaintain (bright yellow)
2  cups of water
   Salt to taste


*P*eel the plaintain and cut each fingers into 3 or 4 pieces. Add salt and water and boil for about 10 minutes or until tender.

Serve with butter or green vegetable stew.

Makes 4 servings.

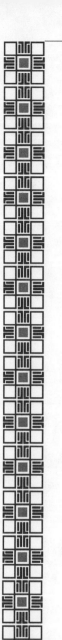

# Baked or Fried Fish With Stewed Gravy

3   pounds of fresh Fish
1   14½ oz. can of Stewed Tomatoes
1   small size Onion
1   cup of Flour
2   cups of Vegetable Oil
1   Maggi or Bouillon cube
½   teaspoon of dry or fresh Pepper (ground)

*S*easonings for Fish: a pinch of black pepper, garlic powder, thyme, curry, etc. Salt to taste

## Baked Fish

*C*lean and season fish.  Bake in oven (400°F) for about
     15 minutes or until cooked.

## Fried Fish

*C*lean and season fish.  Coat with flour and fry till golden brown.

## Gravy

*B*lend stew tomatoes with pepper and ½ of the onion.  Chop the remaining onion.  Heat oil till sizzling hot. Add chopped onion and stir.  Add stewed tomatoes mixture, maggi(bouillon) cube and seasoning.  Reduce the heat and cook for about 10 minutes.  Add salt to taste.  Pour on the side or on top of the baked or fried fish.  Serve with rice.

Makes 4 servings.

# Steam Fish Stew

5   pounds Cat Fish
1   cup of Vegetable Oil
3   cans of 14½ oz Stewed Tomatoes
1   small size Onion (chopped)
2   Maggi or Bouillon cubes
½   teaspoon of dry Red Pepper
2   pinches of Curry and Garlic Powder
    Salt to taste

Clean cat fish, season with salt and steam for about 3 minutes. Heat oil in a large sauce pan until sizzling hot. Add onion, stewed tomatoes, maggi, curry, garlic, pepper and salt. Cook for about 10 minutes, stirring occasionally. Add fish and cook for about 15 minutes. Allow to cool before serving.

Serve with white rice and vegetables.

Makes 4 servings.

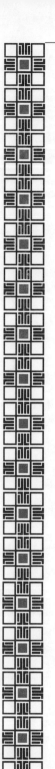

# Chicken or Beef Stew

3   pounds Chicken or Beef
1   cup of Vegetable Oil
3   cans of 14½ oz Stewed Tomatoes
1   large size Onion (chopped)
2   Maggi cubes or bouillon cubes
1   teaspoon of dry Red Pepper
1   tablespoon of chopped Garlic
2   pinches of Curry Powder
1   pinch of Thyme
    Salt to taste

*S*eason Chicken or beef with 20% (⅕) of the onion, garlic and thyme. Add salt to taste. Boil until meat becomes soft. In a large sauce pan heat oil until it becomes sizzling hot. Crush or grind stewed tomatoes. To the oil add onion, stewed tomatoes, maggi, curry, garlic, thyme, pepper and salt. Cook for about 10 minutes, stirring occasionally. Add meat (the meat may be fried or use as cooked) and cook for about 15 minutes. Allow to cool before serving.

Serve on white rice with vegetables.

Makes 4 servings.

# Hot Curried Chicken

| | |
|---|---|
| 1 | whole Chicken |
| ¼ | cup Vegetable Oil |
| 1 | large Onion (sliced) |
| 2 | large Tomatoes |
| 1 | large Green Pepper |
| 1 | tablespoon of Curry Powder |
| 1 | tablespoon of Garlic |
| ½ | teaspoon of Red Pepper |
| ½ | teaspoon of Black Pepper |
| ½ | teaspoon of Thyme |

Clean and cut chicken into bite size pieces. Season with 50% (½) of the garlic, curry powder, onion and Thyme. Add salt to taste. Parboil and cook chicken for about 15 minutes. Saute onion, tomatoes, green pepper, red pepper and black pepper in cooking oil. Add chicken, the remaining garlic, curry powder and thyme. Cook for about 12 minutes stirring at intervals.

Serve with rice and vegetable salad.

Makes 6 servings.

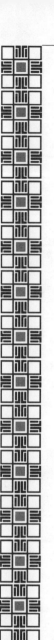

# Spinach/Collard Green Vegetable Stew

2   lbs. of large fresh or dried Shrimp
2   cans of 14½ oz. of Stewed Tomatoes
12  oz of frozen or fresh chopped Spinach
12  oz of frozen or fresh Collard Green
½   cup of Cooking Oil
1   medium size chopped Onion
2   Maggi or Bouillon cubes
1   tablespoon of ground Red Pepper
1   tablespoon of chopped Garlic
1   pinch of Thyme
1   pinch of Ginger powder
1   pinch of Curry powder
    Salt to taste

Clean and parboil shrimp with salt and water in a small pan. Crush stewed tomatoes in a mixing bowl. In a medium sauce pan or skillet heat oil until sizzling hot. Add onion and a pinch of curry powder to oil. Stir and cook for 2 minutes. Add stewed tomatoes, pepper, thyme, ginger and maggi(bouillon) cubes. Cook for about 15 minutes stirring occasional. Add shrimp and cook for another 10 minutes. Clean wash and drain spinach and collard green of excess water. Add spinach and collard green to mixture and cook for 5 minutes. Salt to taste.

Serve with rice or potato pottage.

Makes 6 servings.

A lovely presentation of a West African meal.
(clockwise from left to right)

**Fufu**

**Egusi (melon) Soup**

**Beef Stew**

*A* splendor of color.

(top to bottom)
Meat Pie
Tropical Fruit Salad
Tropical Vegetable Salad
Queens Cupcakes
Chin Chin
Carrot Cake
Meat Pie Bite-Size

*R*obust flavors
and a variety of textures.
(top to bottom)

**Akara**
(African Hush Puppies)

**Seasoned Blackeyed Peas**

**Moin Moin**

*A*romatic
varitey and a bit of spice.

(top to bottom)

Aromatized Goat Meat

Spinach/Collard

Ebe (potato pottage)

*C*olor is abound
in these hardy dishes.

(top to bottom)

Jollof Rice

Tropical Fried Rice with Shrimp

Baked Chicken

Dodo
(fried Plantain )

# Introducing Chin Chin Crispy Pastries

Originating from Africa, now made in the U.S.A.. It is a tasty, crunchy, delicious snack made from pastry. It is immensely popular at weddings and special occasions. Dupsy's Chin Chin is all natural and handmade with tender loving care.

You'll love its exceptionally delicious flavor anytime.

To order or for more information, please call (512) 990-9508.

We sell wholesale to businesses, in bulk for special occasions and retail to individuals.

$\mathcal{F}$ruits and vegetables offer
a variety of color, texture and flavor
while rich in vitamins and minerals.
My recipes will add a delicious
variety to your meals

# ORDER FORM

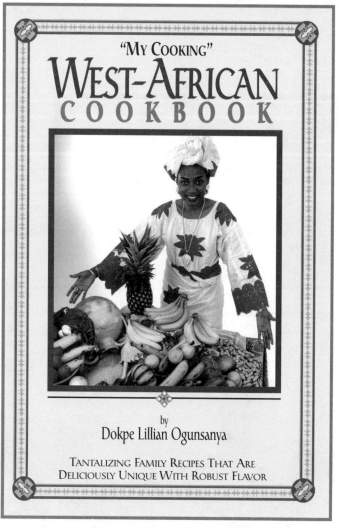

"MY COOKING"
## WEST-AFRICAN
### COOKBOOK

by
Dokpe Lillian Ogunsanya

TANTALIZING FAMILY RECIPES THAT ARE
DELICIOUSLY UNIQUE WITH ROBUST FLAVOR

## My Cooking West African Cookbook

Offers a facinating glimple into the West African kitchens. The book
includes authentic easy to use recipe pages, colorful photos etc.

Name _____

Address _____

City _____ State _____ Zip _____

| Item | Quantity | Cost Ea. | Amount |
|---|---|---|---|
| West African Cookbook | | $12.95 | |
| | | Sub total | |
| Texas Residence add 8.125% Sales Tax | | | |
| Shipping & Handling  3.00 per book | | | |
| | | Total | |

Send Check or Money Order to:    Dupsy Enterprises
P.O.Box 80841
Austin, Texas 787708-80841
U.S.A.

Or Call (512) 990-9508 For More Information

# Okra Soup

("Origin" of Gumbo Soup)

12 oz. of frozen or fresh Okra
1 lb of Beef
1 lb fresh or oven dried Fish
½ lb of fresh or oven dried Shrimp
¼ cup of Palm or Vegetable Oil
2 Maggi or Bouillon cubes
1 tablespoon of dry ground Red Pepper
½ of small Onion (slice or chopped)
1 tablespoon of chopped Garlic
1 pinch of Thyme
  Salt to taste

Season beef with onion, garlic, thyme and salt and put in a 4-6qt sauce pan. Add water and cook on low for about 35 minutes or until meat becomes tender. Chop okra with a knife or in a blender. Clean fish and shrimp. Add oil, shrimp, fish, maggi(bouillon) cubes, pepper and boil for about 12 minutes. Stir in okra and cook for about 7 minutes.

Serve with fufu.

Makes 6 servings.

# Okra Stew

12 oz. of frozen or fresh Okra
1 lb of Beef
1 lb fresh or dried Fish
½ lb or fresh or dried Shrimp
½ cup of Palm or Vegetable Oil
2 14½ oz. cans of Stewed Tomatoes
2 Maggi or Bouillon cubes
1 tablespoon of ground Red Pepper
½ medium Onion (chopped)
1 tablespoon of chopped Garlic
1 pinch of Thyme
   Salt to taste

Season beef with 50%(½) of the chopped onion half, garlic, thyme and salt and put in a 4-6qt sauce pan. Add water and cook for about 35 minutes or until meat becomes tender. Chop okra with a knife or in a blender. Crush stewed in tomatoes a mixing bowl. In a 4-6qt sauce pan heat oil until sizzling hot. Add the remaining onion, stewed tomatoes and pepper. Cook for about 6 minutes. Clean fish and shrimp. Add shrimp, fish, maggi cubes and boil for about 12 minutes. Stir in okra and cook for about 7 minutes.

Serve with yam or rice fufu(see page 43 & 44).

Makes 6 servings.

# Yam Fufu
(pounded yam)

## "Original":

1   medium size tuber of African Yam
6   cups of Water

𝒫eel yam and cut or slice into small pieces. Clean and place into 4qt. pot. Cover with water. Cook until yam becomes tender (can be easily pierced with a fork). Drain excess water and pound with a wooden spoon in a mortar, piece by piece until it forms a mass and becomes a little bit elastic to touch. (An electronic yam pounder may also be used to yield almost the same result). Scoop yam onto a wet plate. Smooth with wet wooden spoon and shape into a round ball.
Serve with green leafy vegetable soup, okra soup or egusi soup.

Makes 2 servings..

## Yam Fufu made Easy!

2   cups of Yam Flour (I recommend "Mimi Yam Powder")
4   cups of Water

𝓑oil water. Reduce heat and Stir (use wooden spoon) in yam powder. Stir constantly to prevent lumps. Cook for about 2 minutes adding more water as needed to achieve the desired texture. Scoop onto a wet plate. Smooth with wet wooden spoon and shape into a round ball.
Serve with green leafy vegetable, okra soup or egusi soup.

Makes 2 servings.

# Rice Fufu

### (Foo Foo)

## "Original":

1   lb of Rice
10  cups of Water
½   teaspoon Salt

*B*oil rice in water and salt for about 45 minutes (cook in a covered pot to expedite the cooking time) or until rice becomes mushy.  Reduce and mash  rice with wooden spoon until it forms a firm mass and becomes a bit stiff.  Scoop into a wet plate. Smooth with wet wooden spoon and shape into a round ball. Serve with green leafy vegetable or okra soup.

Makes 2 servings.

## Rice Fufu made Easy!

2   cups of Rice Powder
4   cups of Water

*B*oil water, stir (use wooden spoon) in rice powder and reduce heat.  Continue to stir until mixture becomes thick in form and forms a mass.   Add more water as needed to acquire desired texture. Scoop into a wet plate.  Smooth with wet wooden spoon and shape into a round ball.
Serve with green leafy vegetable or okra soup.

Makes 2 servings.

# Aromatized Goat Meat

3  pounds of Goat Meat (see introduction)
1  cans of 14½ oz. of Stewed Tomatoes
1  large size Onion (chopped)
1  small Onion (sliced)
2  Maggi or Bouillon cubes
1  tablespoon of dry ground Red Pepper
2  tablespoon of chopped Garlic
1  clove of fresh Garlic
4  pinches of Thyme
2  pinch of Ginger powder
2  pinch of Curry powder
   Vegetable Oil
   Salt to taste

Clean and cut meat into desired bite size pieces. Add ½ (50%) of each ingredient with the exception of the sliced onion, clove of garlic, stewed tomatoes and vegetable oil. Add salt to taste. Boil in a covered medium size pot with plenty of water on high heat for about 1 hour. Reduce heat and cook for about another hour or until meat becomes tender to desired texture. Drain excess fat and water. Fry meat in a shallow pan with very little oil, sliced onion and garlic (this will give the meat flavor and great aroma). Turn over to fry other side. Put aside in a baking pan or dish. Crush the stewed tomatoes put in the fry pan and saute with onion and the rest of the ingredients for about 8 minutes. Pour over meat and cover with aluminum foil. Bake in hot oven for about 5 minutes (this will further "lock" the aroma "deep" into the meat - resulting in great flavor!!). Remove aluminum foil and leave uncovered in oven for another 2 miniuts to allow the meat to brown.
Serve with your favorite dish.

Makes 6 - 8 servings.

# Goat Meat Pepper Soup

3½ pounds of Goat Meat
1   tablespoon of ground Red Pepper
1   small Onion (chopped)
⅓   cup of chopped Tea-Bush leaves
⅓   cup of ground dry Crayfish or Shrimp
2   Maggi or Boullon cubes
    Salt to taste

*C*lean and cut meat into small bite sizes pieces. Add onion, pepper, maggi or bouillon and salt. Boil in a large covered pot with plenty of water on high heat for about 1 hour. Reduce heat and cook for another hour or until meat becomes tender to desired texture. Add more water (about 2/3 of the pot), tea-bush leaves and crayfish or shrimp. Cook for about 15 minutes. Simmer for another 20 minutes.

Serve warm as an apetizer.

Makes 8 - 10 servings.

# African Spiced
# Fried or Baked Chicken

1   whole Fryer Chicken
1   small size Onion (sliced)
1   Maggi or Bouillon cube
1   tablespoon of Garlic
½   teaspoon of Red Pepper
1   pinch of Curry Powder
1   pinch of Thyme
    Salt to taste
    Vegetable oil for frying (optional)

*W*ash and clean chicken. Cut into eight pieces. Add and season chicken with all ingredients except oil. Add very little water and parboil(see glossary) for about 10 minutes. Remove chicken and bake uncovered in the oven at 350° for about 15 minutes or fry in hot oil until brown.

Serve with joll of or fried rice at parties.

Makes 4 servings.

# Spicy Fried Snail
## (Escargot)

10   large Snails (cleaned or dressed)
1   14 oz. can of Stewed Tomatoes
1   medium size Onion
1   teaspoon of chopped Garlic
1   teaspoon of dry ground red Pepper
2   pinches of Curry Powder
     Salt to taste

Snails can cleaned or dressed by doing the following: crack the shells; remove the edible part or flesh (snail meat); wash several times in water to remove the slime (fresh lime cut in halve may also be used to remove slime).

Boil snails covered with salt and water in a medium size pot for about 20 minutes or until tender. Blend ½ of the onion with stewed tomatoes and the red pepper. Chop the remaining onion. Heat oil in a large cooking pot until sizzling hot. Add chopped onion and garlic. Pour in blended ingredients. Add curry powder. Cook/fry (uncovered) on medium heat for about 15 minutes. Add snails and saute on low heat for another 5 minutes. Serve as side dish with rice.

Makes 5 servings.

# SNACKS AND DESSERTS

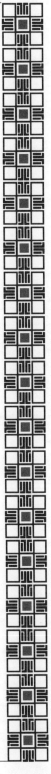

# Puff Puff

3    cups of All Purpose Flour
½   cup of Sugar
1    tablespoon of Yeast
1½  cups of Warm Water
     Vegetable Oil for deep frying

*M*ix yeast in water. Add sugar and allow to stand or ferment for about 15 minutes.  Add flour to mixture and mix.  Cover and let stand for about 30 minutes.  Heat oil until very hot (about 400°.  Put one scoop at a time into oil and deep fry until golden brown.

Makes 20 balls.

# Meat Pie

6 cups of All Purpose Flour
1 lb. of lean Ground Beef
6 oz of melted Butter or Margarine
½ cup of Vegetable Oil
½ teaspoon of Baking Powder
3 pinches of Salt
3 large Potatoes
1 large Onion (chopped)
1 cup of diced or chopped Carrots
1 large Tomato (diced or chopped)
2 Maggi or Bouillon cubes
½ teaspoon of Curry Powder
½ of Black Pepper
2 pinches of Thyme
2 Egg (for glazing)
3 cups of Water

*B*oil meat with ¼ of the chopped onion, 1 maggi cube, and ½ of the thyme, curry and black pepper. Discard excess fat from meat stock. Cut potatoes into small cubes and parboil with a pinch of salt. Saute the remaining onion, tomato, carrots, and meat. Add the remaining thyme, curry maggi cube and black pepper. Allow to cook on low heat for about 10 minutes. Add potatoes and continue cooking for another 10 minutes. Remove from heat and cool. In a large mixing bowl prepare the pie dough (a dough maker or kitchen aid mixer may be use to expedite the process) by rubbing the melted butter or margarine into the flour with finger tips until the mixture resembles bread crumbs. Make a well in the center and pour in 1½ cups of water. Fold in the flour together to form a paste. Do not over handle. Add the remaining water to soften the texture of the dough as necessary. Lightly knead dough and flatten with a rolling pin on a cutting or pastry board (sprinkle flour on board before using). The pastry should be about ½ inch thick. Cut into circles or desired shapes. Smaller sizes are great for cocktails and receptions. Put the cooked meat and vegetables into the center and damp the edge of the dough with water or beaten eggs. Fold to seal and use fork to press down the edges. Brush the top with beaten egg to give a glace finish. Place on cookie or baking sheet. Heat oven to 375° and bake for about 25 minutes or until light brown. Remove from oven and allow to cool before serving.

Makes 12 servings.

# Grilled Meat Kbobs

2   pounds lean boneless Beef
⅓   cup of Vegetable or Olive Oil
4   crushed Maggi or Bouillion cubes
4   large Tomatoes
2   large Onions
2   large Green Pepper
8   large Skewers
    Salt to taste

Clean and cut meat into slices of about ½ inch thick and 2 inches long, season with maggi(bouillion) and salt. Cut onion, tomatoes, and pepper into desired shape (cube or wedge). Place the meat slices alternating with onion, tomatoes and pepper on the skewers. Brush with oil and place on hot grill. Brush with oil at intervals to prevent dryness. Cook until meat becomes tender or to desired texture.

Makes 8 servings.

# Suya
## (Meat On Stick)

1    lb lean boneless Beef
1½  tablespoon of ground roasted Peanut
1½  tablespoon of Vegetable or Olive Oil
1    tablespoon of Ginger Powder
½   tablespoon of dry ground Red Pepper
½   teaspoon of Clove Powder
2    Maggi cubes
4    large wide Skewers

Clean and cut meat into thin flat slices (about ½ inch thick). Mix all ingredients together except oil and meat. Arrange meat on skewers. Coat meat with mixture and brush with oil. Grill until meat is brown on both sides or to desired taste.

Makes 4 servings.

# Yam or Potato Balls

8   large Russet Potatoes or 2½ lbs. African Yam
½   cup of Sugar
1   raw Egg
8   oz of Stewed Tomatoes
⅓   cup of All Purpose Flour
1   small Onion (finely chopped)
½   teaspoon of Red Pepper
1   pinch of Thyme
    Vegetable Oil for deep frying
    Salt to taste

*P*eel and cut potatoes or yams into large chunks. Put potatoes or yams into a 4-6qt. pot, cover with water, add sugar, 3 pinches of salt and bring to boil until potatoes or yams become tender. Drain excess water. Grind stewed tomatoes. Heat 3 tablespoon of oil in a skillet until sizzling hot. Add onion, stewed tomatoes, pepper, thyme and salt to taste. Allow to cook for about 5 minutes. Mash potatoes until smooth. Mix the fried mixture with the mashed potatoes. Mix egg and add to mixture. Roll mixture into small balls, coat with flour and deep fry until golden brown. Drain out excess oil and serve warm or at room temperature.

Makes about 15 balls.

# Tropical Fruit Salad

2   medium seedless Guava (cut into small cubes)
2   fresh Mangoes (slice or cut into cubes)
2   cups of cubed or sliced Pawpaw (Papaya)
2   Oranges (peel and cut into cubes)
2   cups of cubed Pineapple
⅓   cup of Grated Coconut
2   firm Bananas (cut into cubes)
2   Tangerines (peel and cut into cubes)

*Please feel free to add other locally available fruits
for more color and variety.

Syrup Mix:
3   cups of Water
½   cup of Sugar
1   medium Lemon

*C*ombines syrup mix and bring to boil for about 5 minutes.
Allow to cool.  Mix guava, mangoes, pawpaw, orange, pineapple
and tangerine in a large bowl.  Add syrup.  Garnish with grated
coconut.  Chill for about 2 hours.  Add Banana few minutes
before serving.

Makes 6 servings.

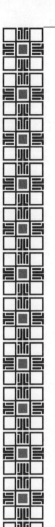

# Plantain Chips

4 pounds Ripe Plantain (bright yellow and firm) or
Unripe Plantain (green). Please note that ripe plantain
taste sweeter than unripe plantain
Vegetable Oil for deep frying
Salt to taste

*P*eel plantain and slice into thin pieces of desired shapes (either round or long across the length).  The thinner the slices of the plantain, the more crispy the texture of the finish product Season slightly with salt.  Heat oil  hot (about 400').  Pour in small quantity at a time and fry plantain until very light brown.  Do not overcook because it can easily  burn. Remove from frying pan or pot and put in a colander to drain excess oil and to cool before serving.

Makes 6 servings.

# Dundun
## (Fried Yam)

2   pounds of African Yams or Russet Potatoes
4   cups of Vegetable Oil for deep frying
    Salt to taste

Peel and wash yam.  Slice into tiny round pieces.  Sprinkle with salt to taste.  Heat oil (about 400').  Fry and cook yam untill light brown.  Avoid overcooking, for it will result in a bitter/sweet taste.
Allow excess oil to drain off and serve warm

Makes 4 servings.

# Mosa
## (Banana Fritter)

2   pounds over-ripe Bananas
1½  cup All Purpose Flour
3   cups of Vegetable Oil
2   medium size Eggs
1   pinch of Salt

*P*eel, mash or beat bananas into paste.  Beat eggs and add salt. Pour egg into banana and mix thoroughly.  Add flour and stir. Heat oil.  Scoop batter with tablespoon or use ice cream scoop and fry until golden brown on both sides.  Drain excess oil and cool slightly before serving.

Makes 4 servings.

# Rice Cake

2½ cups All Purpose Flour
1   cup of Rice Flour
1   cup of Sugar
2   4 oz. sticks of Margarine or Butter
3   large Eggs
¼   cup Milk
1   tablespoon of Vanilla Extract
½   teaspoon of Baking Powder

*H*eat oven to 350°.  Generously grease bottom and sides of baking pan.  Sprinkle lightly with flour.  In a mixing bowl mix margarine or butter and sugar.  Add eggs, vanilla extract and beat in a large brown on low speed for 45 seconds or until texture becomes smooth.  Add  all purpose flour, rice flour and baking powder.  Beat on medium speed for about 2 minutes or whisk/hand mix with large spoon for about 3½ minutes.  Pour into pan and bake for about 35 minutes or 45 minutes for bunt cake pan.  Cake is done when it passes the toothpick test (stick a toothpick into the center of the cake, the cake is done if it comes out clean).  Cool completely on wire rack before serving.

Makes 6 servings.

# Sausage Rolls

5  cups of All Purpose Flour
4  oz. country style hot, mild or regular Sausage
4  oz. of melted Butter or Margarine
½  teaspoon Baking Powder
2  pinches of Salt
1½ cups of Water
1  Egg (for glazing)

*P*repare dough (a dough maker or kitchen aid mixer may be use
to expedite the process) in a mixing bowl by rubbing the melted
butter or margarine into the flour with finger tips until the mixture resembles bread crumbs.  Make a well in the center and pour
in 1 cup of water.  Fold the flour together to form a paste.  Do
not over handle.  Add the remaining water to soften the texture of
the dough as necessary.  Lightly knead dough and flatten to ½"
thick with a rolling pin on a cutting or pastry board (sprinkle flour
on board before using).  Take tablespoon of sausage, dip in flour
and form into a roll(log shaped). Cut the dough into long oblong
strips(about 2"x3") or big enough to cover the rolled sausage
pieces.  Damp the edges of the dough with water.  Place sausage
in cut dough strips and fold the dough over the sausage.  Press
the edges together for a zip fold.  Cut rolls into smaller sizes.
Make holes with fork at the top of rolls to allow the release of
steam while cooking.  Brush the top with beaten egg to give a
glace finish.  Place on cookie or baking sheet.  Heat oven to 350°
and bake for about 20 minutes until light brown.

Makes 8 servings.

# Carrot Cake

| | |
|---|---|
| 2 | cups of All purpose Flour |
| 1 | cup of Sugar |
| 3 | oz. of Butter or Margarine |
| ½ | cup of Raisins (optional) |
| ½ | cups of grated Carrots |
| 2 | large Eggs |
| 1 | tablespoon of Baking Powder |
| ½ | teaspoon of Lemon Juice |
| ½ | teaspoon of Cinnamon |
| 2 | pinches of Nutmeg |
| 1 | pinch of Salt |

*M*ix butter or margarine with sugar until it becomes creamy. Add beaten eggs and lemon juice. Add and mix, the flour, baking powder, cinnamon, nutmeg, and salt. Add raisin and carrots and mix gently. Heat oven to 350°. Generously grease bottom and sides of baking pan, then sprinkle lightly with flour. Bake for about 35 minutes until golden brown. Cake is done when top springs back when touched in the center.
Cool before frosting or serving.

Makes 10 servings.

# Queens Cup Cake

2 cups of All Purpose Flour
1 cup of Sugar
4 oz. of Butter or Margarine
2 medium size Eggs beaten
1 tablespoon of Baking Powder
1 teaspoon of grated Lemon Peel
2 oz. of Currants (optional)
1 pinch of Salt

*M*ix butter or margarine with sugar in a medium mixing bowl until it becomes creamy. Add beaten eggs. Add and mix in flour, lemon peel and currants. Heat oven to 350°. Put paper cups or liners in cupcakes pan. Fill liners or paper cups half full with batter. Bake for about 20 to 30 minutes or until golden brown. Cake is done when toothpick inserted in center comes out clean. Cool before frosting or serving.

Makes 8 servings.

# Gurudi

(Traditional Coconut Biscuits)

2½ cups of finely grated Coconut
⅓  cup of Sugar
1   cup of Cassava Starch
⅓  Water or Coconut Milk
2   pinches of Nutmeg

*M*ix water or coconut milk with sugar and starch in a medium
mixing bowl . Add the grated coconut. Mix very well and add
nutmeg. Spread the mixture on a baking sheet and cut into
desired shapes (squares or round) and sizes. Bake on medium
heat (about 320°) until light brown and very crispy.
Allow to cool before serving.

Makes 4 servings.

# Coconut Toffee

2   cups of freshly extracted Coconut Milk
2   cups of Sugar
2   teaspoon of finely chopped fresh Ginger
½   teaspoon of Lime or Lemon Juice
½   cup of Water

Boil sugar and water.  Add coconut milk, lime or lemon juice and ginger.  Cook and stir until mixture becomes thick and brown.  Pour onto a baking sheet lightly greased with butter or margarine.
Allow to cool before serving or storing.

Makes 8 servings.

# Rice Pudding

| | |
|---|---|
| 5 | oz of Rice |
| 3 | cups of Coconut Milk |
| ⅓ | cup of Sugar |
| 2 | tablespoons of Coconut Flakes |
| ½ | teaspoon of Vanilla Extract |
| ½ | teaspoon of Nutmeg |
| ½ | teaspoon of Cinnamon Spice |

Boil rice in coconut milk in a covered pot on low heat until rice becomes very soft. Add sugar, vanilla extract and nutmeg. Stir, cover and cook on low heat for about 3 minutes. Pour into a dish and cool. Sprinkle top with cinnamon powder.
Refrigerate (optional) for few minutes before serving.

Makes 6 servings.

# Tapioca Pudding

½   cup of Tapioca
3   cups of Coconut Milk
¼   cup of Sugar
2   pinches of Salt
    Dash of Nutmeg for garnishing


Soak Tapioca in coconut milk for about 10 minutes in a 2qt pan. Add sugar and salt. Bring to boil and reduce heat. Cook on low heat for about 5 minutes. Allow to cool. Garnish with a dash of powdered nutmeg. Serve hot topped with milk or pour into a bowl and chill for desert.
Allow to cool. Garnish with a dash of nutmeg for garnishing.

Makes 4 servings.

# Doughnut

5    cups of All Purpose Flour
1½  cups of Sugar
4    oz. of Butter or Margarine
2    tablespoons of Baking Powder
3    large size Eggs
½    tablespoon of Milk
     Vegetable Oil for deep frying


Mix flour, baking powder and butter or margarine.  Add sugar.
Stir in beaten eggs and milk.  Mix and cut into shape with a
doughnut cutter.  Heat oil until very hot (about 400°).  Deep fry
for about 3 minutes or until golden brown.  Allow to cool before
serving.
Sprinkle top with a little bit of cinnamon sugar.


Makes 8 servings.

# Boiled Groundnuts
### (Peanuts in the Shell)

12  oz. of raw Peanuts in the shell
Water
Salt to taste

*B*oil peanuts in the shells, covered with water in cooking pot with the lid on. Add salt to taste. Cook for about 40 minutes. Reduce heat and cook for another 10 minutes or until tender. Sample the nut to test for texture. Most people prefer the nuts to be very soft (avoid over cooking). Drain out excess water. Allow to cool before serving. Nuts are cracked open with fingers or with nutcracker before eating.

Makes 6 servings.

# Traditional
# Groundnut Butter
### (Peanut Butter)

9    oz. of unsalted roasted shelled Peanuts
     Salt to taste

*A*dd a little salt to peanuts and warm in a frying pan over low heat for about 3 minutes.  Pour into a blender and blend until smooth.  Allow to cool.  Pour into an air tight container and refrigerate.
Serve with bread.

Makes 12 servings.

# Corn on the Cob and Coconut

6  ears of fresh Corn
1  medium size fresh Coconut
2  tablespoons of Butter or Margarine (optional)
   Salt to taste

*R*emove corn husk(skin or outer coverings and silk).

Immerse corn on the cob in water and salt in a large covered pot.

Cook for about 45 minutes or until corn becomes tender.  Dab

with butter or margarine.  Break and remove coconut from shell.

Wash with water and cut into small pieces.

Serve corn with coconut on the side.

Makes 6 servings.

# Kuli Kuli
## (Peanut Balls)

2½  pounds of roasted skinless Peanuts
2    cups of Vegetable Oil
¼    cup of Sugar
1    cup of Warm Water

*B*lend peanut and sugar in a medium size mixing bowl until smooth.  Knead and squeeze to extract the peanut oil. Add a little bit of warm water as you squeeze (to maintain texture).  Repeat the process until most of the peanut oil are extracted.  Scoop and shape the peanut mixture into bite size round balls.  Heat oil (about 400') in a small frying pan.  Fry the peanut balls until golden brown.  Drain out excess oil.  Allow to cool before serving. Makes about 15 balls.

# Burns

4 cups of Flour
2½ oz of Butter or Margarine
1 cup of Sugar
2 tablespoons of Baking Powder
¼ cup of Milk
1 large size Egg
2 pinches of Salt
Vegetable Oil for deep frying (optional for baking)

Mix flour, baking powder and salt in a large mixing bowl. Rub in butter or margarine. Add sugar. Beat egg and mix with milk. Make a well in the center of the dry ingredients in the mixing bowl. Pour in egg mixture. Mix the ingredients until you get a consistency. Use a medium size scoop or tablespoon to put the mixture into a hot oil (about 400°) and deep fry until golden brown or bake in hot oven (350°) for about 12 minutes or until golden brown.

Makes 10 servings.

# Chukchuk
## (Coconut Balls)

1   cup of Coconut Flakes or freshly grated coconut
3½ spoons of Sugar
2   medium size Egg yolks

*M*ix the coconut, sugar and egg yolks.  Form into bite size balls. Roll each ball in flour and place on baking sheet.  Bake in oven at 350° for about 5 minutes or until golden brown.
Allow to cool before serving.

Makes 6 - 8 balls.

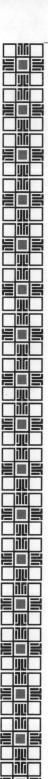

# Homemade Fruit Cake

4½ cups of all purpose Flour
2    cups of Sugar
2    cups of Butter or Margarine
8    large size Eggs
3¼ tablespoon of Baking Powder
1½ cups of your choice of mixed fruits (fresh or dried)
¼   cup of Milk
1    tablespoon of Vanilla Extract
½   teaspoon of Cinnamon powder
1    whole nutmeg

*M*ix sugar and butter or margarine until soft and creamy in a medium size mixing bowl. Beat eggs and add to mixture. Continue mixing on a low speed. Mix flour and baking powder in another bowl. Grate in the nutmeg. With a spatula or wooden spoon, fold in flour mixture into the creamy mixture. Add vanilla extract and mixed fruits. Generously grease and lightly flour baking pan. Pour in the mixture and bake in hot oven (350°) for about 25 - 35 minutes or until golden brown. Cake is done when top springs back when touched in center. Cool for about 10 minutes in pan. Remove from pan and cool completely before frosting or serving.

Makes 10 servings.

THE ETHNIC RECIPES
IN THE NEXT SECTION
ARE FROM PEOPLE OF
VARIOUS REGIONS OF
WEST AFRICA.

THEY HAVE A
RICH ROBUST FLAVOR
THAT WILL MAKE A MEAL
UNIQUE & SPECIAL

# ETHNIC
# SPECIALTIES

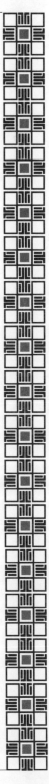

# Obe Efo Elegusi (Egusi

(Melon Vegetable Soup)
One of the favorite of the Yoruba tribe of Western Nigeria.

2   lbs of Beef
1   lb of fresh or dried Fish
½   lb fresh or dried Shrimp
½   lb Stock Fish (cut into small pieces)(see glossary)
1   cup of dry-ground Egusi (melon seed)(see glossary)
⅓   cup of Palm or Vegetable Oil
1   cup chopped Spinach
1   cup of chopped Collard Green
1   medium size Onion
2   large size Tomatoes
1   tablespoon of dry ground Red Pepper or
    2 large size fresh Red Peppers
2   cubes of Maggi or Bouillion
1   tablespoon of chopped Garlic
½   teaspoon of Thyme
    Salt to taste
    Broth  (from boiled beef)

Season meat with salt, garlic, thyme and ¼ of the onion in a 4qt. pan.  Add water and boil for about 40 minutes or until meat becomes tender (save broth).  Boil stock fish with salt and water until soften to taste.  Clean fresh fish and shrimp and salt lightly (or soak dry shrimp and dry fish in hot water with salt for about 2 minutes before use).  Blend onion, tomatoes and pepper.  Add meat broth to egusi and allow to sit for about 3 minutes before use.  Heat oil and fry blend ingredients for about 5 minutes.  Add Egusi, meat,  shrimp and stockfish.  Cook for about  20 minutes stirring as it cooks. Add fish, maggi and salt to taste.  Cook on covered for about 10 minutes.  Add  spinach, collard green and cook for about 5 minutes.
Serve with fufu, pounded yam or rice.

Makes 8 servings.

# Ofe Owerri

One of the favorite of the Ibo tribe of Eastern Nigeria.

2   lbs dried or fresh Beef
1   lb dried Fish
½   lb Stock Fish (cut into small pieces)(see glossary)
⅓   cup of Palm Oil
¼   cup of ground Crayfish
1½  cup of Ugu (Pumpkin leaves)
⅓   cup of shredded Okazi leaves
1   tablespoon of dry ground Red Pepper
2   cubes of Maggi or Bouillion
2   cups of Water
    Salt to taste

Season meat with salt and boil until tender.  Clean and boil stockfish with salt and water until soften to taste.  Break dried fish into large chunks and soak in hot water with salt for about 2 minutes before use.  Put the water, palm oil and pepper in a pot and bring to boil.  Add stock fish, meat, dried fish, crayfish, and pepper.  Cook for about 15 minutes.  Stir.  Add maggi or bouillion, okazi and ugu leaves.  Cook for another 5-7 minutes.
Serve with pounded yam.

Serves 6.

# Edikang Ikong

A favorites of the Efik/Ibibio tribes from Southern Nigeria

1½ lb of Beef
1   lb dried Fish
1   lb of Stock Fish (see glossary)
½   lb of Cow Skin (optional)
½   lb of Beef Shank (see glossary)
½   lb of Beef Tripe
1½ cup of Periwinkle
2   cups of palm oil
¼   cup of ground Crayfish
2   cups of chopped Ugu (Pumpkin leaves)
2   cups of chopped Water Leaves (Spinach)
1   large Onion
3   cubes of Maggi or Bouillion
1½ tablespoon of dry ground Pepper
    Salt to taste

*C*ut beef meat into large chunks.  Clean and cook beef, beef shank, tripe in a large pot until tender (season with salt and few slices of onion).  Remove beef and tripe.  Add stock fish and cow skin(optional) to the beef shank in the large pot.  Cook for about 35 minutes or until meat becomes tender.  Add beef, tripe, pumpkin leaves and water leaves(spinach).  Cook for about 10 minutes stirring occasionally.  Stir in oil, fish, pepper, crayfish, periwinkle, and maggi.  Cover the pot and cook for about 20 minutes.  Stir and salt to taste.
Serve with fufu (p.43&45).

Makes 8 servings.

# Miya Yakwa

One of the favorites of the Hausa tribe of Northern Nigeria.

1½ lbs of Beef
½ cup of shelled raw ground Peanuts
5 tablespoon of Vegetable Oil
1 lb Yakwa leaves (can subsitute collard greens)
2 large Tomatoes
1 large Onion
2 cubes of Maggi or Bouillion
4½ cups of Water
   Salt to taste
   Broth (from boiled beef)

Clean and cut beef into chunks. Season with salt and ⅕ of the onion. In a 4qt. pan boil for about 40 minutes or until tender (save broth). Chop tomatoes and onion. Heat oil and stir fry tomatoes and onion for about 5 minutes. Cover pot and allow to cook for about 15 minutes. Add meat and broth. Stir, add water and allow to boil for few minutes. Mix the peanut with a little water and add to the soup. Add maggi or bouillion cubes and the cleaned shredded Yakwa leaves. Stir and cook for about 6 minutes.
Serve with rice fufu or tuwo acha.

Makes 6 servings.

# Banga Soup

## (Palmnut Soup)

A favorite of the Itshekiri people from Mid-Western Nigeria.

2   lbs of Banga (palmnut or palmfruit)
2   lbs of Beef
1½ lbs of dried Fish
1   lb of dried Shrimp
⅓  cup of ground dried Crayfish(popcorn shrimp)
½  cup of chopped Okra (optional)
1   medium size Onion
1½ tablespoons of dry ground Pepper
1   tablespoon of Beletientien
½  tablespoon of Ikrabo
½  tablespoon of ground Atariko
½  tablespoon of Rigije
2   cubes of Maggi or Bouillion
6   cups of warm Water
    Salt to taste

*B*oil the palmnut for about 50 minutes (skin must be very tender). Drain out water. Mash with hand or pound in a mortar to extract the juice from the palmnut, you can also buy the canned palmnut fruit juice. Pour the mashed palmnut into a colander and strain out the juice into a pot. With the colandar still in place over the pot, pour the 6cups of warm water over palm nut to remove any remaining juice, set the pot with water and juice aside. Cut meat into chunks, season and boil with salt and ½ of the onion for about 20 minutes. Clean fish by soaking in hot water with salt for about 3 minutes. Pour the strained palmnut juice into a large pot (clay cooking pot is preferred because it expedite the cooking time and produce a thicker tastier soup). Bring to boil and add meat, fish, shrimp, onion (finely chopped), beletientien, atariko and rigije. Cook for about 20 minutes. Add maggi and okra and allow to cook for about 7 minutes. Add salt to taste. Serve with Eguobobo (pounded boiled plaintain with cassava starch).

Makes 8 servings.

# Owo

A favorites of the Urhobo people of Mid-Western Nigeria.

1½ lbs dried Meat (Beef can be cut boiled and dried in oven to achieve the same result)
1   lb of Smoked Fish
½   cup of Palm Oil
½   lb of dried Periwinkle
3   tablespoons of dried ground Crayfish
1½  tablespoons of Cassava Starch
1   teaspoon of African Potash
2   cubes of Maggi or Bouillion
4   pods of Egidije
1½  tablespoons of dry ground Red Pepper
    Salt to taste

*P*our hot water over dried meat with salt and soak for about 5 minutes.  Clean and put into a large pot.  Boil for about 8 minutes.  Add crayfish, ground egidije, pepper and maggi or bouillion cubes.  Boil for about 7 minutes.  Mix starch in cold water and pour immediately into the soup, stirring as you pour to avoid lumps.  Add potash, palm oil and salt to taste.

Serve with boiled yam, plaintain or starch.

Makes 8 servings.

# BEVERAGES

# Tropical Fruit Punch

8   cups of Pineapple Juice
2   cups of Guava Juice or Nectar
1   cup of Mango Juice or Nectar
1   cup of Orange Juice
1   cup of Lemon Juice
1   large size of fresh Lemon (sliced)
2   liters of Lemon or Lime Soda
    Mint leaves (optional)

*P*our and mix all juice in a large bowl.
Add lemon or lime soda.  Clean mint leave.  Garnish edge of bowl
with mint leaves and the sliced lemon.

Chill and serve.

Makes 8 servings.

# Pineapple Drink

4   cups of Pineapple Juice
2   cups of Water
8   Cloves spice
½   of medium size fresh Lemon
     Sugar to taste (optional)

Mix juice and water together in bowl.  Add clove spice and squeeze in the juice from the fresh lemon.
Chill and serve.

Serves 4.

# Pawpaw Drink

1   medium size Pawpaw (Papaya)
4   medium size Limes or Lemons
2   cups of Water
    Sugar to taste (optional)

*W*ash pawpaws and remove the skin. Cut open to remove seeds. Chop pawpaws and put in a blender. Puree and sieve(strain) out the pawpaw juice. Add water and squeeze in the lemons or limes. Add sugar to taste.
Chill before serving.

Makes 4 servings.

# Ginger Drink

1   lb of fresh Ginger
¼   cup of Cloves
2   medium size fresh Lemons or Limes
8   cups of Water
    Sugar to taste

*W*ash ginger and put in a blender and blend on medium speed for 1 or 2 miniutes, pour into a 4qt. pan.  Add water, cloves, and sugar.  Boil for about 8 minutes.  Allow to cool and sieve(strain) out the liquid.  Squeeze in lemon or lime juice and chill before serving.

Makes 4 servings.

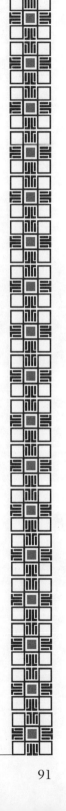

# Glossary

| | |
|---|---|
| Akara | Fried Blackeyed Peas (fritters) paste mix with onion, pepper and salt. Deep fry in hot oil. |
| African Potash | Native salt used for flavoring and to expedite the cooking time for some foods. |
| Atariko | Small seeds with very strong scent use as spice in palm fruit/palm nut soup. |
| Banga Soup | Soup dish prepared with palm fruit pulp |
| Beletientien | Dried ground herb |
| Blackeyed Peas Paste | To prepare Blackeyed Pea paste: Soak the peas or beans in water for about 3 hours. Remove the skin by rubbing the peas vigorously between your palms. Drain off the floating hull or skin. Repeat the process several times until majority of the peas are hulled. Remove the remaining individually. Grind or blend into paste and use. Alternatively, there are commercial powered Blackeyed Peas. I recommend "Mimi Worldwide Foods Blackeyed Pea Powder." |
| Black Pepper | Small black dried seeds usually ground before use. African black pepper are similar to European and American black pepper. |
| Boil | Cook food by bringing water or liquid to boiling point |
| Colander | Sieve with large perforations |
| Cooking Oil | Corn oil, Cranola oil, Fish oil, Groundnut (peanut) oil, Olive oil, Soybean oil, Vegetable oil, etc. |

| | |
|---|---|
| Dodo | Fried Plantain |
| Dried Crayfish | Dried shrimp |
| Dry Fish | General term use for fish which has been preserved by heat. |
| Efo | Yoruba term use for green leafy vegetables |
| Egidije | Small brown seeds used as spice for palm fruit/palm nut soup |
| Egusi | melon seed |
| Fold | Overturning gently in repeated motions |
| Frying | Deep Fry: fry food immersed in frying pan half to two-thirds full of hot cooking oil. Shallow Fry: fry food in shallow pan with little cooking oil. Food is usually turned over to fry other side. |
| Fufu | Also referred to as foo foo. It is a general term for most thickened carbohydrate foods made from yam, cocoyam, cassava, potato, rice, etc. |
| Groundnut | Peanut |
| Maggi cube | Bouillon cube made of evaporated seasoned meat extract |
| Okazi - Ibo | (Eastern Nigeria) name for the dry leaves of a creeping plant. |
| Palm Oil | Red color oil extracted from palm fruits. |
| Parboil | Boil briefly. |

| | |
|---|---|
| Pepper | Comes in different varieties and color. The red dry pepper categories are available whole or ground. The red dry ground pepper are very hot and more popular. The fresh pepper are some times not as hot as the red dry pepper, but they add more flavor and color to the food. The red pepper (fresh and dried) belongs to the Capsicum family. |
| Plaintain | Large "banana" with green color when unripe and yellow color when ripe. Ripe plantain tastes sweeter than unripe plantain. |
| Simmering | Cook in liquid below boiling point. |
| Smoked Fish | Fish that is thoroughly smoked to give flavor. |
| Stock Fish | Completely dried fish imported to the West-African countries.. |
| Saute | Fry in very small amout of cooking oil. |
| Snail | Escargot |
| Steaming | Cooking by moist heat form boiling water. |
| Stewing | Slow method of cooking by boiling or with simmering heat in a small amount of liquid. |
| Stewed Tomatoes | Combination of sliced tomatoes, tomatoes juice, onion, celery and bell pepper. |
| Tea-Bush Leaves | Pungent herb |
| Yam | African Yam: Root vegetable common in the tropics but, mainly native and cultivated in Africa. The yam species in West-Africa are mainly white and yellow. It is a good source carbohydrate and contains some protein. The Russet Potatoe can be subsituted in it's place. Sweet Potato is referred to as yam in the United States and should not be used. |

# Index

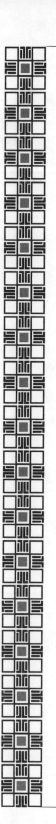

# Your Favorite Recipes

Recipe Name                                                    Page No.

_____  _____
_____  _____
_____  _____
_____  _____
_____  _____
_____  _____
_____  _____
_____  _____
_____  _____
_____  _____
_____  _____
_____  _____
_____  _____
_____  _____
_____  _____

Notes:

# Your Favorite Recipes

Recipe Name                                    Page No.
_____        _____
_____        _____
_____        _____
_____        _____
_____        _____
_____        _____
_____        _____
_____        _____
_____        _____
_____        _____
_____        _____
_____        _____
_____        _____
_____        _____
_____        _____

Notes:

# Your Favorite Recipes

Recipe Name                                                Page No.

_____        _____
_____        _____
_____        _____
_____        _____
_____        _____
_____        _____
_____        _____
_____        _____
_____        _____
_____        _____
_____        _____
_____        _____
_____        _____
_____        _____
_____        _____

Notes:

# Your Favorite Recipes

Recipe Name                                    Page No.

_____    _____

_____    _____

_____    _____

_____    _____

_____    _____

_____    _____

_____    _____

_____    _____

_____    _____

_____    _____

_____    _____

_____    _____

_____    _____

_____    _____

_____    _____

Notes:

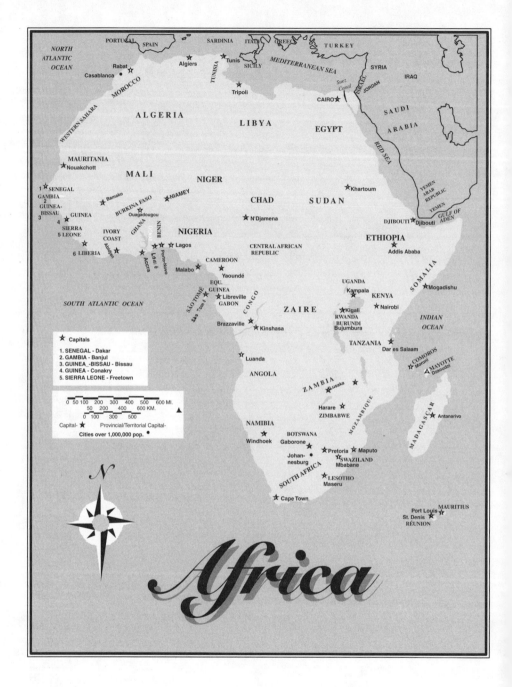

# THIS PAGE IS DEDICATED TO
# THE PEOPLE AND CONTINENT OF
# AFRICA